Mel Bay's First Lessons Ukulele

by Jerry Moore

CD CONTENTS

<table>
<tr><td>1</td><td>Tuning [0:48]</td><td>18</td><td>Camptown Races (melody) [0:28]</td></tr>
<tr><td>2</td><td>Three Blind Mice [0:20]</td><td>19</td><td>Do Lord (harmony F) [0:24]</td></tr>
<tr><td>3</td><td>Twinkle Twinkle Little Star [0:29]</td><td>20</td><td>Do Lord (harmony G) [0:24]</td></tr>
<tr><td>4</td><td>Beautiful Brown Eyes [0:24]</td><td>21</td><td>Do Lord (harmony B♭) [0:25]</td></tr>
<tr><td>5</td><td>Stars & Stripes Forever [0:11]</td><td>22</td><td>Do Lord (melody F) [0:20]</td></tr>
<tr><td>6</td><td>Mary Had A Little Lamb [0:36]</td><td>23</td><td>Do Lord (melody G) [0:19]</td></tr>
<tr><td>7</td><td>Three Blind Mice (picking) [0:19]</td><td>24</td><td>Do Lord (melody B♭) [0:19]</td></tr>
<tr><td>8</td><td>Three Blind Mice (strumming) [0:20]</td><td>25</td><td>My Wild Irish Rose (harmony B♭) [0:42]</td></tr>
<tr><td>9</td><td>Mary Had A Little Lamb (melody) [0:37]</td><td>26</td><td>My Wild Irish Rose (melody B♭) [0:27]</td></tr>
<tr><td>10</td><td>Mary Had A Little Lamb (harmony G) [0:35]</td><td>27</td><td>Swanee River (harmony C) [0:35]</td></tr>
<tr><td>11</td><td>Mary Had A Little Lamb [0:34]</td><td>28</td><td>Swanee River (melody C) [0:35]</td></tr>
<tr><td>12</td><td>Mary Had A Little Lamb 2nd position [0:34]</td><td>29</td><td>Swanee River (harmony F) [0:37]</td></tr>
<tr><td>13</td><td>Beautiful Brown Eyes (harmony) [0:23]</td><td>30</td><td>Swanee River (melody F) [0:35]</td></tr>
<tr><td>14</td><td>Row Row Row Your Boat [0:12]</td><td>31</td><td>When the Saints Go Marching In (harmony) [0:22]</td></tr>
<tr><td>15</td><td>Crawdad Song (harmony) [0:23]</td><td>32</td><td>When the Saints Go Marching In (melody) [0:18]</td></tr>
<tr><td>16</td><td>Crawdad Song (melody) [0:21]</td><td>33</td><td>Amazing Grace (harmony) [0:31]</td></tr>
<tr><td>17</td><td>Camptown Races (harmony) [0:27]</td><td>34</td><td>Amazing Grace (melody) [0:24]</td></tr>
</table>

It doesn't get any easier.....

1 2 3 4 5 6 7 8 9 0

Visit us on the Web at www.melbay.com — E-mail us at email@melbay.com

Table of Contents

Introduction

Welcome to the wonderful world of the ukulele. If you already play the uke, then you are aware of the fun and enjoyment that this unique little instrument can bring. If you are just beginning, then you have made a very wise choice. Anyone can play the ukulele. No musical knowledge or special talent is required, and you don't have to sing or read a note of music.

Most people believe that the ukulele is strictly a harmony instrument, meaning that its primary function is to be strummed sweetly while you or others sing, whistle, hum, or accompany other musical instruments. Actually, the uke is a marvelous melody instrument. You will soon play both the harmony and melody to the songs in this book. You will learn how to hold it, tune it, strum it, pick it, form chords, play in different keys, and delve into the sacred area of "higher position chords."

The Basics

The ukulele is a small, lightweight, guitar-like instrument, usually with four strings. In most cases, ukes are made of wood, but plastic has been used successfully in their construction. There are four types:

Soprano   smallest, nylon strings, approximately 21 inches long.

Concert   slightly larger, nylon strings, same tuning as soprano

Tenor   larger than concert, slightly different string configuration

Baritone   largest, tuned same as top four strings of a guitar

Parts and Pieces

For use with this book, we will use a soprano ukulele. First, it is necessary to become familiar with the structure of the ukulele. Most ukes look like the one shown here. Starting with the top of the uke you find the:

Head: contains the pegs used for holding the strings and tuning the instrument.

Pegs: used to tune the strings by tightening or loosening each string. Some pegs are positioned through holes drilled in the head, others use guitar-like tuning pegs, positioned on sides of the head.

Strings: are attached to the pegs through holes in the peg shafts. The strings are numbered 1 through 4, beginning with #1 on the bottom and moving upward.

Nut: a slightly raised plastic or wooden bar, located at the base of the head, with shallow slots cut to accomodate the strings.

Neck: also known as fretboard or the fingerboard. The long, thin section of the ukulele.

Frets: usually thin, raised strips of metal. The fingerboard is covered with frets, 12 or more

Position Marks: small dots found on the 5th, 7th, 10th, 12th and 15th frets of the fingerboard. Used for locating desired position of chords or notes.

Body: a.k.a. sound box. Connected to the neck. The quality of sound, resonance and beauty is found in the quality and construction of the sound box.

Sound Hole: usually found in the top of the body, approximately one inch and a half in diameter. Its purpose is to allow the beautiful sounds to escape from the sound box.

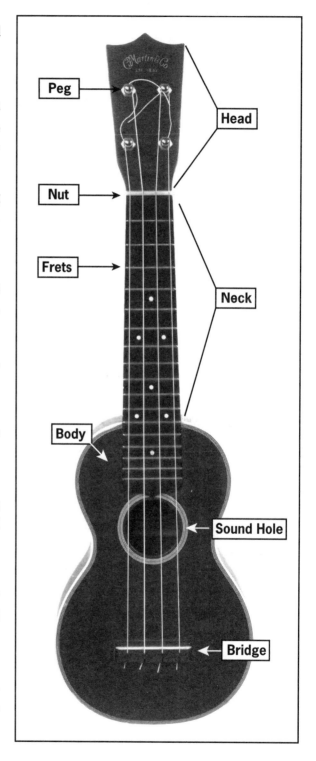

Bridge: located near the bottom of the body. This is where the strings are attached, then run to the pegs so they can be tuned.

Holding the Uke

The ukulele is so small and lightweight that you can play it while standing, sitting, lying on your back or even hanging upside down. Many prefer to play it while standing, but it is a bit easier to grasp and brace while sitting.

1. Hold it on a slight upward angle, such that it feels comfortable.

2. Press your right forearm against the lower front portion of the soundbox, holding it snug against your body.

3. Use your left hand to pull a slight tension on the top end of the uke to counterbalance the pressure of your right forearm.

4. Smile... unlike the sourpuss in the picture (oops, that's me). Remember, the uke is supposed to be the instrument of fun.

The thumb plays an important role in chording. The thumb position for most chords will be on the back of the neck where it will act as a pivot.

With the thumb pressing on the back, the tips of the fingers press the strings against the fingerboard between the the frets—with a pincer-like action. Try this a few times. It will probably feel awkward. With practice comes the "touch."

Tuning the Uke

The strings can be tightened or loosened by turning the pegs on the head. Before attempting this feat, you should probably become familiar with the diagram (below) which depicts the position of the nut, the strings and the frets, and also is the foundation for the chord diagrams which will be used later in the book:

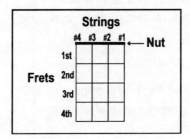

There are several ways to tune your ukulele:

1. The CD furnished with this book

For use with this book, we will tune the ukulele to **GCEA**. Just follow the instructions given on the CD. Since you will not have your CD always available, and ukes do go out of tune at the most inappropriate times, there are other methods.

2. Tuning with a pitch pipe

This little device, usually made of plastic, is composed of four tuned pipes that match the notes for the four strings of the uke.

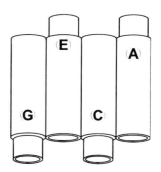

   1. Blow lightly into the **G** pipe several times, until the note becomes familiar.

   2. Turn the peg for the #4 string, continuing to pick this string and alternately blowing the **G** note on the pitch pipe until the note on the string exactly matches the note on the pipe. Test it several times to be sure of a match.

   3. Repeat the procedure for each of the other strings.

3. Tuning with a piano

If you have access to a piano, imagine that the following diagram is the middle of the piano keyboard.

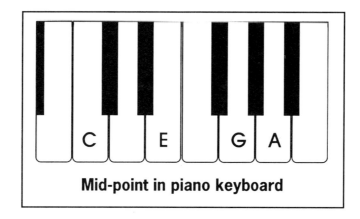

Mid-point in piano keyboard

   1.) Find the mid-point of the piano keyboard (26 white keys from either end). Locate **G**, which is two white keys to the right of the mid-point. Play this key several times until the note becomes familiar.

   2.) Turn the peg for the #4 string and continue to pick this string until the note matches the **G** note on the piano.

   3.) Using the piano keys, repeat the same procedure for each of the other strings, **C** then **E** then **A**.

4. Tuning with another ukulele

If you have access to another uke which is tuned **GCEA**, you can use it to tune your ukulele.

   1.) Turn the peg for the #4 string, continuing to pick this string until the note matches that made by picking the #4 string on the other ukulele.

   2. Repeat the same procedure for each of the other strings.

5. Tuning string to string

This could be the most important method of all. There will be times when you have no CD, pitch pipe or other instrument available. You need to memorize the **Tuning Diagram** shown here. If any of the strings are still in tune, you can use the string-to-string relationship to tune the rest of the strings. If all of the strings are out of tune then you have to take your best guess for one of the notes—usually the #4 or **G** string. The procedure would be as follows:

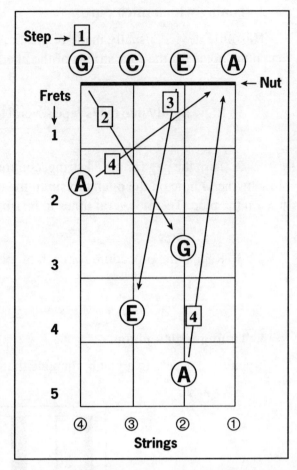

1. *Tune the #4 string (G)*—turn the peg for the #4 string, continuing to pick this string until you feel that the note is as near the **G** note as you can recall.

2. *Tune the #2 string(E)*—notice on the Tuning Diagram that the 3rd fret of the **E** string has a circled **G**. This designates the location of the note **G** on that string. While holding the uke with the thumb in the proper position, place the tip the second (middle) finger, left hand, on the #2 string, 3rd fret. Turn the peg for this string while picking the string occasionally and still pressing on the 3rd fret, until the note matches the #4 string. When these notes match, the #2 string will be tuned to **E**.

3. *Tune the #3 string(C)*—to do so, you have to match the **E**, or #2 string (which you just tuned) to the 4th fret of the #3 string(C). Turn the peg for the #3 string while pressing the 4th fret of the same string, picking the string until the note matches your #2 string(E).

4. *Tune the #1string(A)*—You have two options; you can tune it with the #4 string(G), 2nd fret, or the #2 string(E), 5th fret, or both.

    a. Turn the peg for the #1 string(A) while picking it, until the note matches that made by picking the #4 string(C), 2nd fret.

    b. Repeat the procedure in a. using the #2 string (E) 5th fret.

Using the **Tuning Diagram**, try to match all of the notes as shown, beginning with the **G** and **E** strings, then the **E** and **C** strings, finally the **G** and **A** or the **E** and **A** strings.

Chords and Music

The more proficient you become in forming chords, the better your music will sound. Here is a sample of a chord diagram as used in this and many other books. This is the **C Chord**:

The C Chord

Pick up your uke and assume the proper position. Place the tip of your third finger, left hand on the #1 string, 3rd fret, as shown in the picture. Release the chord, then re-form it. Keep doing this until the movement feels natural. Run the fleshy tip of your right thumb across all four strings. Each string should give a nice, clear note.

1. Introduction to Strumming

Strumming your ukulele can be done with either the thumb, the index finger, all four fingers, or the thumb and one or more fingers. An entire section of the book is devoted to strumming (pages 12 - 14) but you need to become familiar with the basics to proceed from here.

Thumb- You can run the fleshy tip of your thumb across the strings slowly, as you did trying out the **C Chord**, or you can strum it across the strings quickly on a downward stroke. You can make repeated downstrokes or strums as you play songs. Practice this a few times using the **C Chord**.

Index finger- Using the either the fleshy tip of your index finger (first finger), or, for a crisper sound, use the fingernail, strum across all four of the strings quickly on a downward stroke. Once you have crossed all of the strings, you can make another downstroke, or bring your finger back across all four strings with an upstroke. Practice these techniques a few times with the **C Chord**. Next, let's see how you can count as you strum.

2. Treble Clef and Time Signature

Below is a diagram showing a hypothetical music staff, illustrating a Treble Clef and Time Signatures:

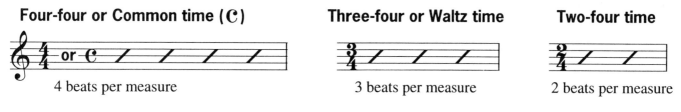

Four-four or Common time (C)	**Three-four or Waltz time**	**Two-four time**
4 beats per measure	3 beats per measure	2 beats per measure

/ = one stroke or strum of the thumb or finger

Playing the **C Chord** your strums on the ukulele would be as follows:

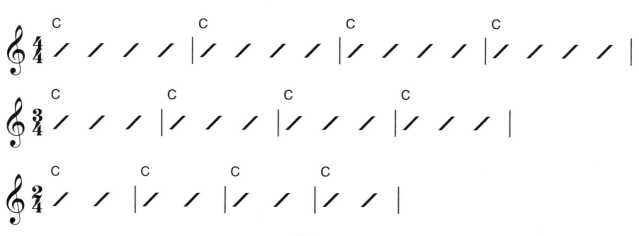

First song:

Everyone knows *Three Blind Mice*. By fudging a bit it can be played using only one chord. Since we now know one chord, the **C Chord**, let's use it. Form the chord, turn to the next page, then play this very simple song using the different strums and rhythms we have just covered.

Three Blind Mice

Three blind mice, three blind mice, see how they run, see how they run. They all ran af - ter the farm - ers wife, who cut off their tails with a carv - ing knife. Did ev - er you see such a sight in your life as three blind mice?

3. More Chords

The next two chords will be the **F Chord** and the **G7 Chord**.

The F Chord

The G7 Chord

Practice forming these two chords, switching back and forth between these and the **C** chord. Remember to use the thumb as a fulcrum to rotate the left hand, and try to keep your fingers as vertical as possible to avoid contact with other strings.

Second song   Let's try a simple song using the three chords **C**, **F**, and **G7**, *Twinkle, Twinkle, Little Star*. As before, use the basic strums and rhythms. Try to make the chord transitions quickly enough to keep the rhythm constant. If you are brand new to the ukulele, it may take some time to get it working right, but work on it until it feels right. It will be worth the effort.

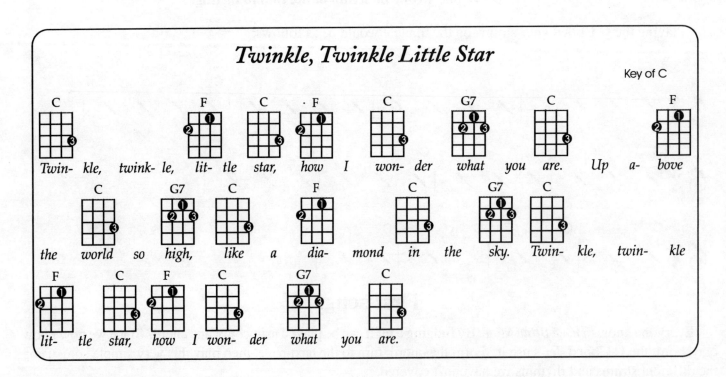

Twinkle, Twinkle Little Star

Key of C

Twin- kle, twink- le, lit- tle star, how I won- der what you are. Up a- bove the world so high, like a dia- mond in the sky. Twin- kle, twin- kle lit- tle star, how I won- der what you are.

4. Barre chords

A barre chord is a chord which uses one finger to cover all or most of the strings across one fret. For example, the **D7** chord, using either the first finger or second finger, left hand to make the barre.

The D7 Chord

Notice that the finger of the left hand covers all of the strings across the 2nd fret. Try forming this chord both ways. Pick each string individually to make sure your barre is making good contact with the fret board.

5. Chords with multiple fingering positions

Occasionally, a chord which we use can be played with more than one set of finger positions. For example, the **D** chord. Here are six variations:

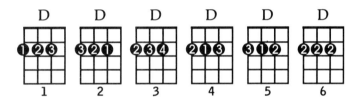

These are all the same chord. Give them a try. Remember to use the left thumb as a pivot, and try to get good finger contact on all of the strings.

The form of the **D** chord we will be using is #6. The secret to making this barre chord is to bend the second finger, left hand, enough so it will completely clear the #1 string, and still exert enough pressure on the other strings to get a clear sound from each string.

The D Chord

6. The killer chord

Absolutely no relationship to Jerry Lee Lewis. This "killer" is the **B-flat Chord**. It is tough to master, but it is a dynamite chord. Try to form it a few times. Don't push too hard with the first finger, you will find that very little pressure is needed.

The B♭ Chord

There are also two optional finger configurations for this chord. Give these a try.

7. The country chord

Country, cowboy, western, hill-billy or whatever. Hank Williams wanna-bes wind up playing songs which begin with the **G Chord**.

The G Chord

It can also be played as a barre chord, as shown here. This configuration is easier to incorporate into **melodies**.

8. Types of chords

There are several types of chords that can be used for playing the ukulele. Following is a partial list of the chord types:

1. Major Chords
2. Minor Chords
3. Dominant Seventh Chords
4. Augmented Chords
5. Diminished Seventh Chords
6. Dominant Seventh Chords with Raised Fifth
8. Dominant Seventh Chords with Lowered Fifth
9. Minor Seventh Chords
10. Major Sixth Chords
11. Minor Sixth Chords
12. Dominant Ninth Chords

For this book, we will be using **Major Chords**, **Minor Chords** and **Dominant Seventh Chords**. Chord Charts for all twelve of the chords in each of these three categories are found on pages 34 to 36. Do you need to memorize every chord in the charts? The answer is no, but it wouldn't hurt to learn as many as possible.

Look through the charts and try forming some of these chords.

How about another song? Let's play *Beautiful Brown Eyes*, using the chords **G**, **C** and **D7**—with the **G** and **D7 Chords** in two different configurations. In the first, we use the **G Chord** without a barre, and the **D7 Chord** with the second finger, left hand as the barre. Try this first version a few times.

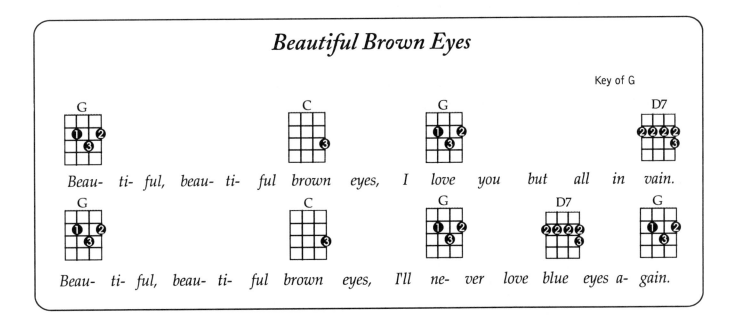

Playing the same song in the second configuration, notice that both the **G Chord** and the **D7 Chord** use the first finger, left hand as a barre across all four strings. Give this second version a few tries.

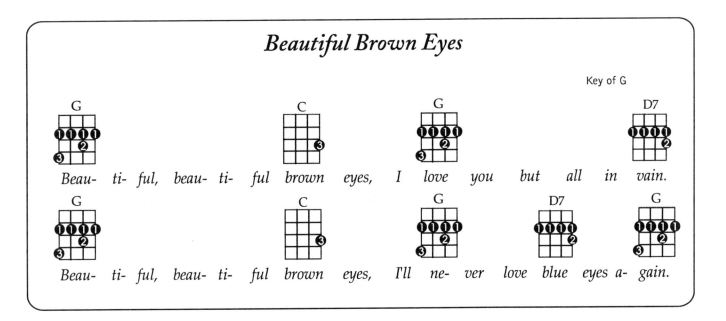

11

Strumming

If you have had the pleasure of listening to some of the great ukulele players, then you are aware of the awesome array of strumming techniques that can be used on a uke. You, too, should be able to create some pleasant sounds. Strumming can be done with either the thumb, the fingers, or a felt pick.

1. Thumb strumming

So far you have been using a very basic strum, passing the fleshy portion of your thumb slowly across the four strings. We call this the Simple Thumb Strum.

Simple Thumb Strum

Although this is the most basic strum, you will find it useful no matter how proficient you may become on the ukulele. You can enhance it by running your thumbs across all four strings *without pausing for each string*. Try it. Vary the speed and rhythm.

Next, we advance a step further with the Full Thumb Strum.

Full Thumb Strum

Just like getting the most out of a golf shot, the action will be all in the wrist. Your arm doesn't have to go up and down as you strum. You simply move your thumb across the strings by rotating your wrist. After you feel comfortable with the **down-strokes**, reverse the procedure for the **up-stroke**. Go lightly on the **up-strokes** since you will be striking the strings with your thumb-nail. For practice, switch back and forth between the <u>Simple Thumb Strum</u> and the <u>Full Thumb Strum</u>.

2. Finger Strumming

Most of your uke strumming will be with your first finger, right hand—commonly referred to as your index finger.

Down-stroke

1.) As with the thumb strum the action will be primarily in the wrist. Begin the **down-stroke** with the index finger about an inch above the #4 string.

2.) You can strike the strings either with the fingernail or the fleshy tip of the finger. The latter provides a softer sound.

3.) The **down-stroke** ends about an inch below the #1 string, and then reverses course.

Up-stroke

1.) The **up-stroke** follows the same path as the **down-stroke**.

2.) The **up-stroke** ends in about the same position in which the **down-stroke** began. Strumming will then be continuous **up/down strokes**.

3. Variations

Down-up-down

Let's alter the basic strum by adding an additional **down-stroke** at the end of the sequence. In other words—**down-up-down**, **down-up-down**... etc. Try pausing briefly between the sequences, vary the speed—fast, slow.

Down-strokes only

Occasionally, strumming with repetitive **down-strokes** provides a nice effect. For instance, there may be a particular part of a song where you would like to put a little emphasis. Switch to **down-strokes only** for that part of the song, then back to your regular strum.

Up-strokes only

Since your finger or thumb will be hitting the #1 and #2 strings first, you will notice a different effect with **up-strokes only**. As with **down-strokes only**, you can use it for emphasis, lead-ins, or just for an occasional change of pace.

4. Combinations

Up to now we have used the thumb or index finger alone for strumming. By using them in combinations, you will find a new world of strumming sounds:

1. First the index finger crosses the strings on a **down-stroke**.

2. The thumb follows immediately on the same **down-stroke**.

3. Finish with an **up-stroke** with the finger.

You can have fun with this combination using partial strokes:

1. Strum all the way across with the finger on the **down-stroke**, but only across the #4 and #3 strings with the thumb.

2. On the **up-stroke** cross only the #1 and #2 strings with the finger.

> When you become more proficient with the combination technique, throw in a few picks on individual notes when playing either the the harmony or melody to a song.

5. Tremolo

Tremolo means the quick repetition of a single note on a stringed instrument. You strum very short, rapid strokes, either with your finger, thumb, or combination, across one or more strings on the ukulele.

> Try to concentrate your tremolo on the string which contains the note for that particular chord in a song. A good tremolo is very impressive.

6. Felt picks

For a nice, soft picking or strumming sound some ukulele players use a felt pick. Picks are about an inch long and are held between the thumb and index finger of the right hand. The strumming stoke would be similar to the finger strum.

Picking

In this section of the book, we discuss picking techniques, using the thumb, one finger alone or in combination with the thumb. Although picking is most useful for hitting notes in **melodies**, a few notes picked while you are playing **harmony** can add to the tune.

1. Thumb picking

The picture shows the hand position for thumb picking, which will be **down-strokes**. You will selectively pick one string at a time with a **down-stroke** using the fleshy part of your thumb. In this picture, the #4 string is being picked.

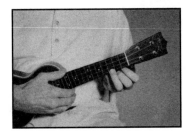

The note to be picked in each chord will be designated by an "x" beneath the proper string on the chord diagrams (see arrows). In the first diagram you will pick the #4 string open. In the second diagram, you will pick the #3 string while your second finger, left hand presses the #3 string against the 2nd fret. To avoid touching an adjacent string (muting), keep the finger as vertical as possible while maintaining good contact.

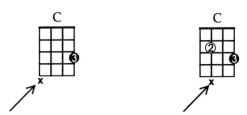

Exercise: Let's try an easy exercise using the thumb picking technique. Below you see seven chord diagrams, with **x**'s located beneath a string on each chord. Form the **C** chord and pick each designated string for each chord in succession from left to right.

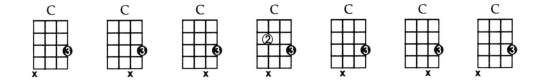

Continue to pick these seven chords. Vary the speed, vary the rhythm, pick softly, and then increase the loudness. Practice until the transition between notes is smooth and consistent.

Congratulations. You have just played the first seven notes of *When Irish Eyes are Smiling.*

2. Finger picking

Most picking is done with the index, or first finger. It is easier to reach the #2 and #1 strings **E** and **A**, by picking with your finger. In this case, the motion will be a very short **up-stroke**, with either the fleshy tip of the finger, or the nail. The picture shows the #1 string being picked with the index finger.

3. Thumb and finger synchronous picking

This technique is analogous with the term "pincer." The first picture shows the thumb picking the #4 string with a **down-stroke** as the index finger picks the #1 string with an **up-stroke**. **Any two strings can be picked simultaneously**.

Here is a short verse of *Stars and Stripes Forever* you can play using the **thumb and finger synchronous picking** technique. Use your thumb to pick the strings that have a "T" beneath them while simultaneously picking the string that has an "F" beneath it. Continue to pick both strings on the chord diagram for each lyric until you come to a chord change, and then do the same for each new chord. It will help to listen to the CD.

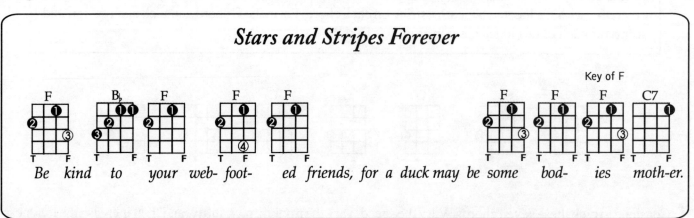

Stars and Stripes Forever

Be kind to your web- foot- ed friends, for a duck may be some bod- ies moth-er.

You should hear the melody coming out a little as you are picking.

Try using this picking technique on the songs you have used in the book so far. You don't have to use it for an entire song, but an occasional pincer may be a pleaser.

Harmonies and Melodies

1. Harmony

As mentioned earlier in the book, when you play **harmony**, you will be accompanying singing, whistling, humming, or another musical instrument. You will be primarily strumming, and chord changes should be minimal. The chord diagram will appear above the lyric, as it has been in the songs done so far in this book. The sample song below is *Mary Had a Little Lamb*, in the Key of **C**. Forgive the use of such basic songs, but they are easy to grasp, and expedite the learning process.

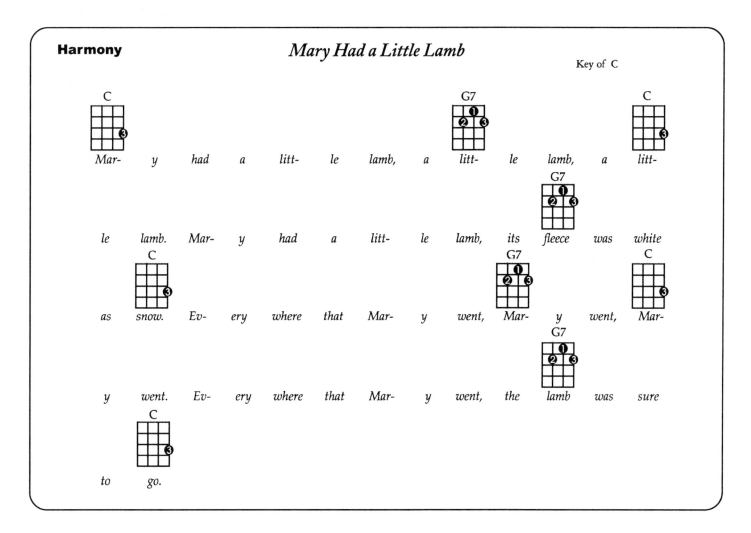

2. Melody

Now, we will be breaking new ground. Playing **melody** means playing every note in a song. In effect, you will be playing ukulele solos. All of the songs in the book from this point on will be shown in both **harmony** and **melody** format. The chords will appear <u>beneath</u> the lyrics, and the string which has the specific note for each lyric has a small "x" below it on the chord diagram.

There are basically three methods for playing **melodies**:

    1. **Picking only-** all notes picked on individual strings, using either thumb or first finger.

    2. **Combination of picking and strumming-** can be picked or strummed or combination of both.

    3. **Chord solos-** strummed only, all notes found on the #1 string. (Will not be covered in this book).

3. Picking only- using *Three Blind Mice*, with only one chord, the **C Chord**.

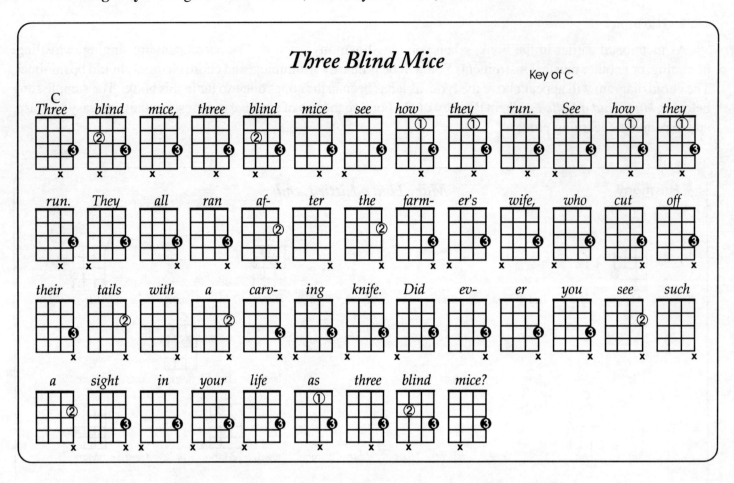

Three Blind Mice

Key of C

3. Combination of picking and strumming- using *Three Blind Mice*, with three chords, **C**, **F** and **G7**.

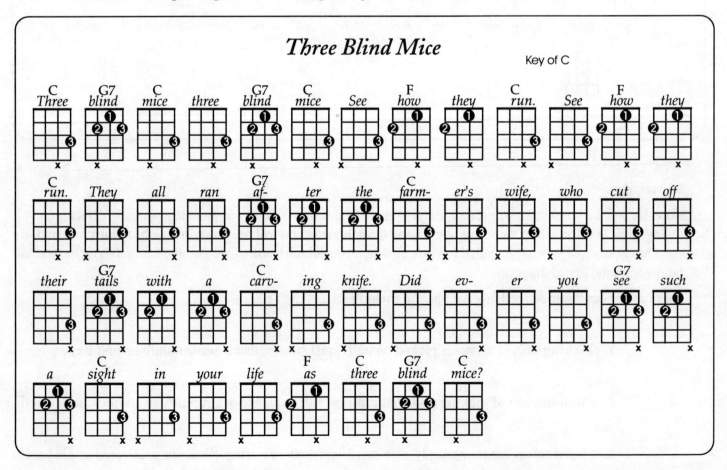

Three Blind Mice

Key of C

18

You should by now be aware that to achieve some of the notes in a **melody**, you have to take some liberties with the chords. For example, in the single chord version of *Three Blind Mice*, you:

1. Used another finger to "roam" and locate the note, as shown here with first and second finger, left hand:

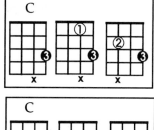

2. Lifted a finger off of the fretboard to locate a note, as shown here using the second finger, left hand, or by lifting the third finger and leaving the string open :

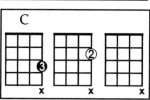

On page 16 you played *Mary Had a Little Lamb* as **harmony**. Here is the same song played as a **melody** using the **Combination of picking and strumming** method. Notice how the first finger, left hand is lifted to form a note in the **G7 Chord**:

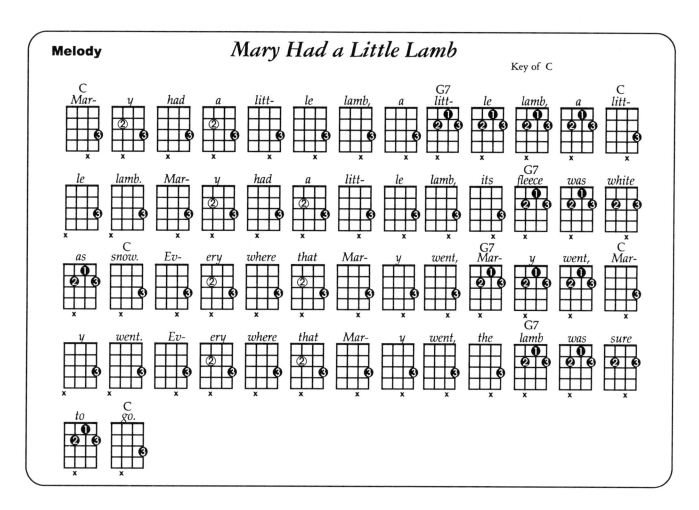

Once more, you have to remember we are using very basic, simple songs to demonstrate these techniques. Before moving on, play these tunes a few times using different strums, varying the rhythm and speed and combinations of picking and strumming. A rule of thumb for melodies:

The melody to almost any tune can be found within or around the chords used to play the song.

Keys

Playing the ukulele in the right key is as important as singing in the right key. As you know from the **Chord Charts**, found on pages 34 through 36, there are twelve major chords and twelve minor chords.

Each of these has its own "**Key**" which consists of two major chords (or minor chords) and one dominant seventh chord.

We will focus primarily on the **Major Keys**. If you read music, you will recognize the "key signature" on sheet music at the beginning of a song. Usually, but not always, the last chord of a song will be the key. Some song books will have the key designated near the title of the song.

Study the **Key Chart** on page 37 for a minute. See if you can determine a pattern for each type of chord. They seem to flow up the keyboard. You are already familiar with all of the chords which make up four of the keys, as shown here:

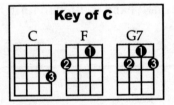
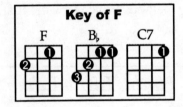
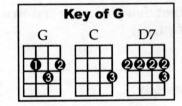

1. Transposing

This is a fancy word which simply means to change the key in which you play a song. For example, we have played *Mary Had a Little Lamb* in the key of **C**. Let's try it now in the key of **G**. You will see that the **G Chord** replaces the **C Chord**, and the **D7 Chord** replaces the **G7 Chord**.

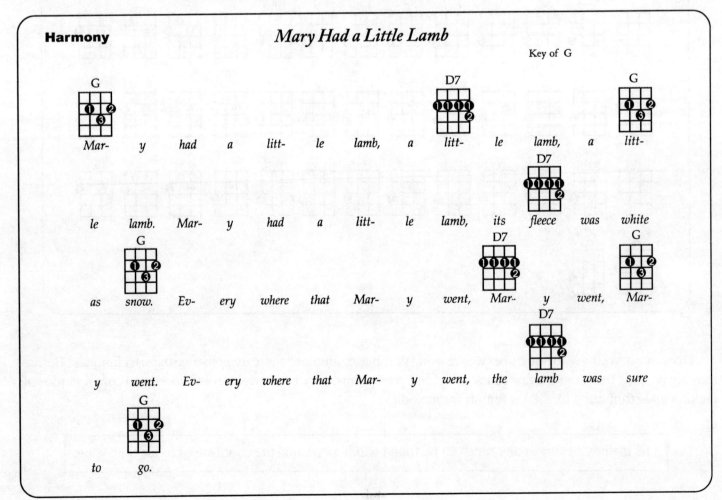

Now let's transpose the same song to the key of **F**. Play it a few times.

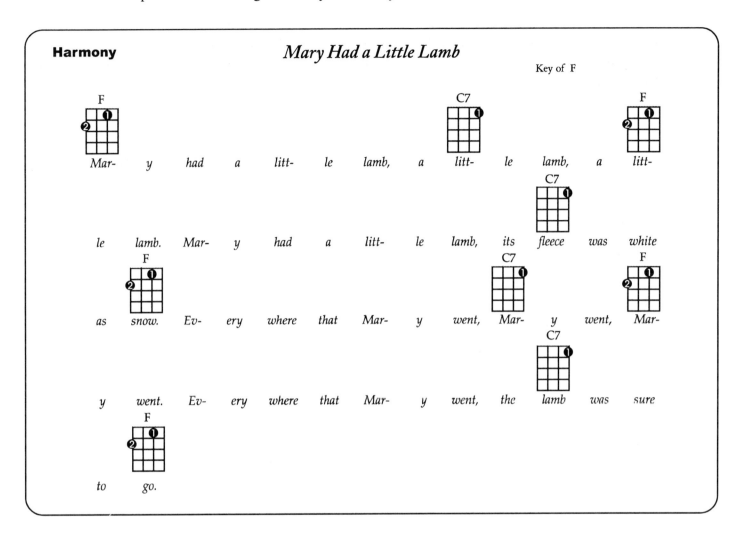

2. How to use the Key Chart for Transposing

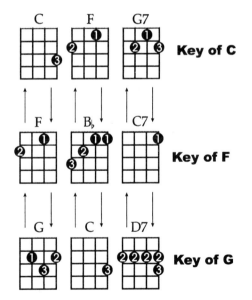

Observe the diagram shown here. If you follow the arrows you will notice that when you transpose (change to a different key) the first chord of one key replaces the first chord of the key being replaced, the second chord for the second chord, and the third chord for the third.

Any key can be substituted for any of the other keys on the **Key Chart**.

Position

All ukulele chords can be played in different positions on the keyboard. The chords you have played so far have all been in the **1st position**. They can go up to **2nd**, **3rd**, **4th** and even **5th position**. The chord fingerings change with each position change. All major, minor and dominant seventh chords are shown **1st**, **2nd** and **3rd position** in the **Chord Position Charts** found on pages 38 to 40.

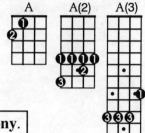

Shown here is the **A Chord** in three positions. Try forming and strumming each of these chords. Listen closely for a nice harmonic resemblance. The important fact is:

> You can play all chords in any position when playing a song in **harmony**.

On the previous page we played *Mary Had a Little Lamb* in the key of **F**. Let's do the same song, in the same key, but use a mixture of **2nd** and **3rd position** chords:

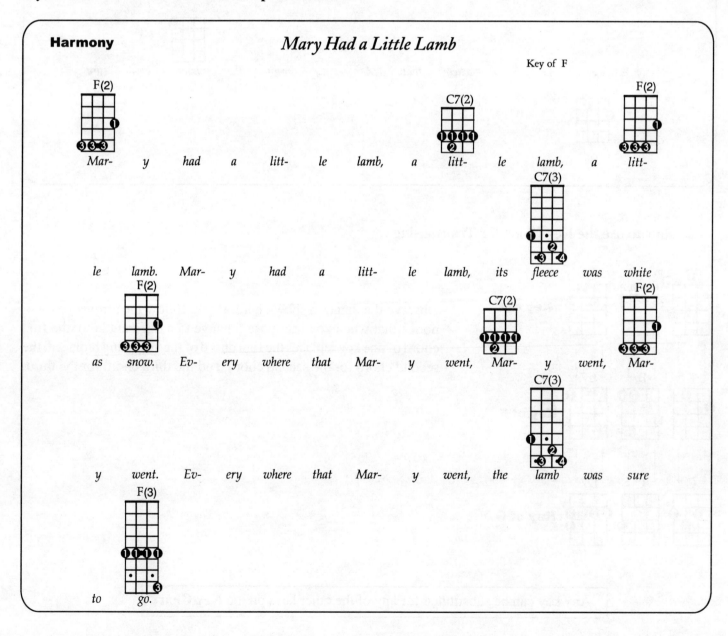

22

Add-ons

Occasionally you can enhance a chord by adding an extra note, usually with the fourth or "pinky" finger. A good example is the **A Chord**. Another is the **F Chord**.

The **C Chord** in **2nd position** also works well.

Below is a **harmony** version of *Beautiful Brown Eyes* in **C** using **2nd** and **3rd position** chords, using the pinky to enhance the **C Chord** in **2nd position**, **C(2)**.

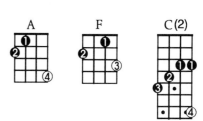

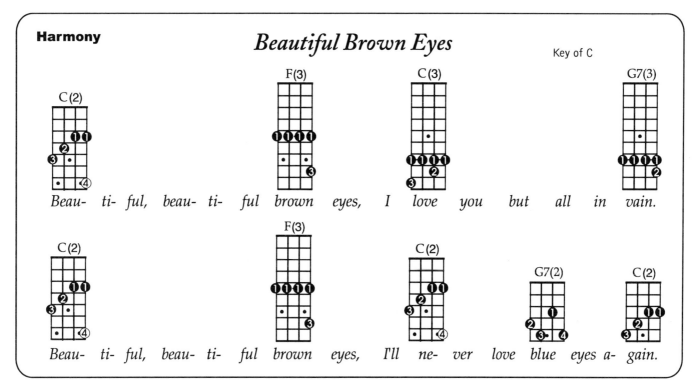

Finally, let's do a **melody** with higher position chords using **add-ons**, *Row, Row, Row Your Boat* in the key of **F**. Remember that the string containing the note for each chord is designated with the "x." You can use **picking**, **picking and strumming**, **tremolo** or try selectively strumming one or two strings instead of all four.

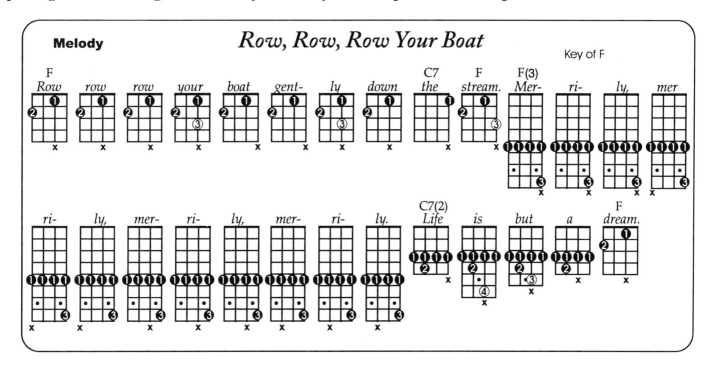

This concludes the instructional portion of the book. Following are songs to play using your new skills, and charts which were referred to in the book. Enjoy your ukulele—it is a marvelous little instrument.

Songs

Harmony

The Crawdad Song

Key of **F**

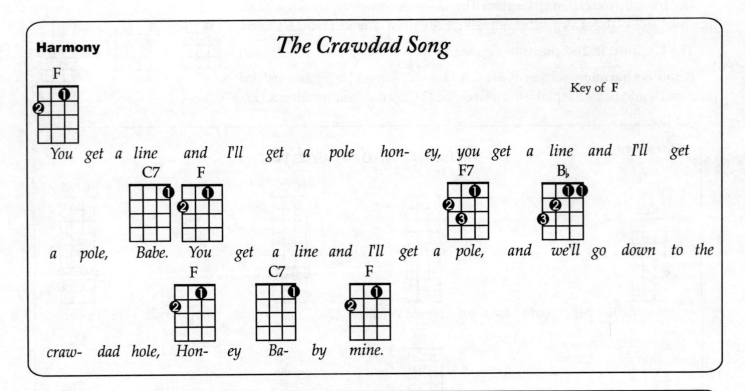

You get a line and I'll get a pole hon- ey, you get a line and I'll get a pole, Babe. You get a line and I'll get a pole, and we'll go down to the craw- dad hole, Hon- ey Ba- by mine.

Melody

The Crawdad Song

Key of **F**

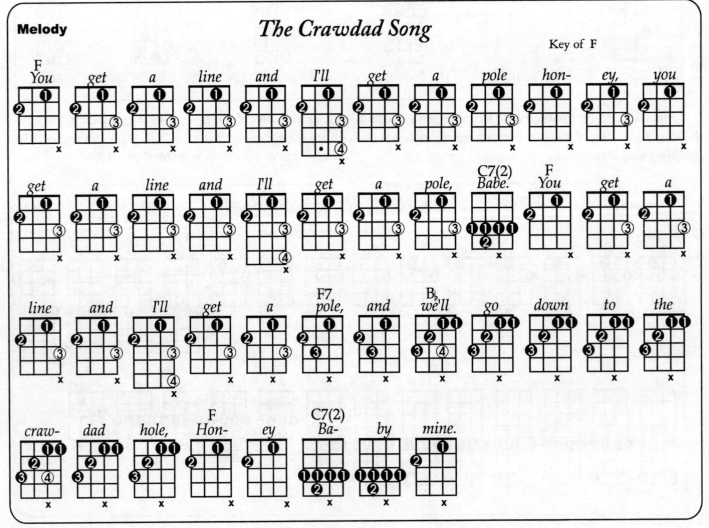

You get a line and I'll get a pole hon- ey, you get a line and I'll get a pole, Babe. You get a line and I'll get a pole, and we'll go down to the craw- dad hole, Hon- ey Ba- by mine.

24

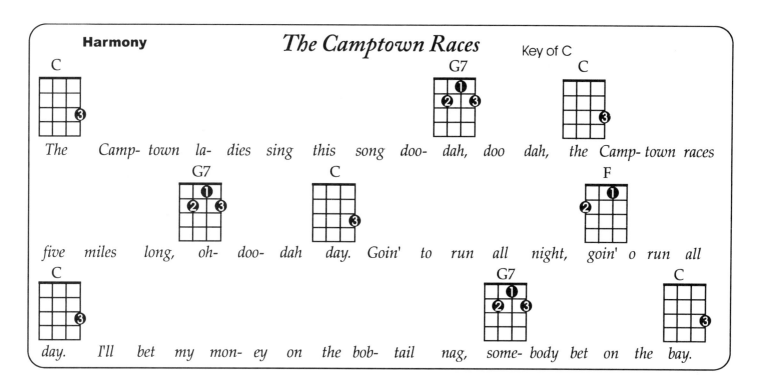

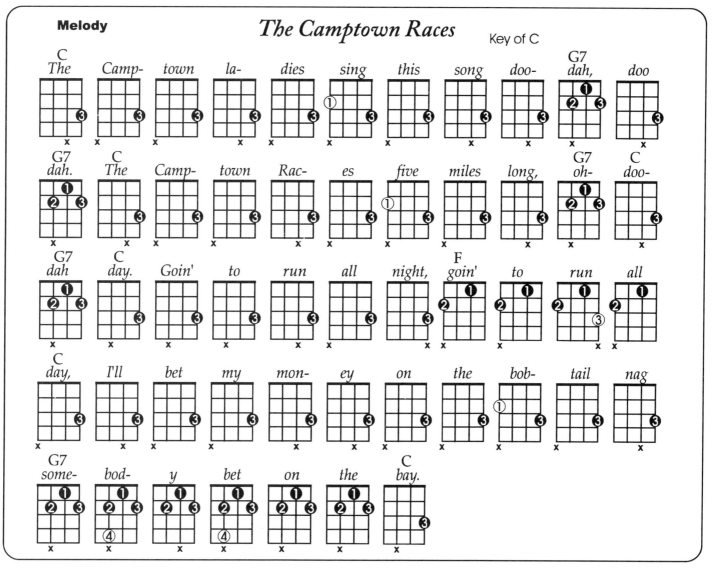

25

Do Lord

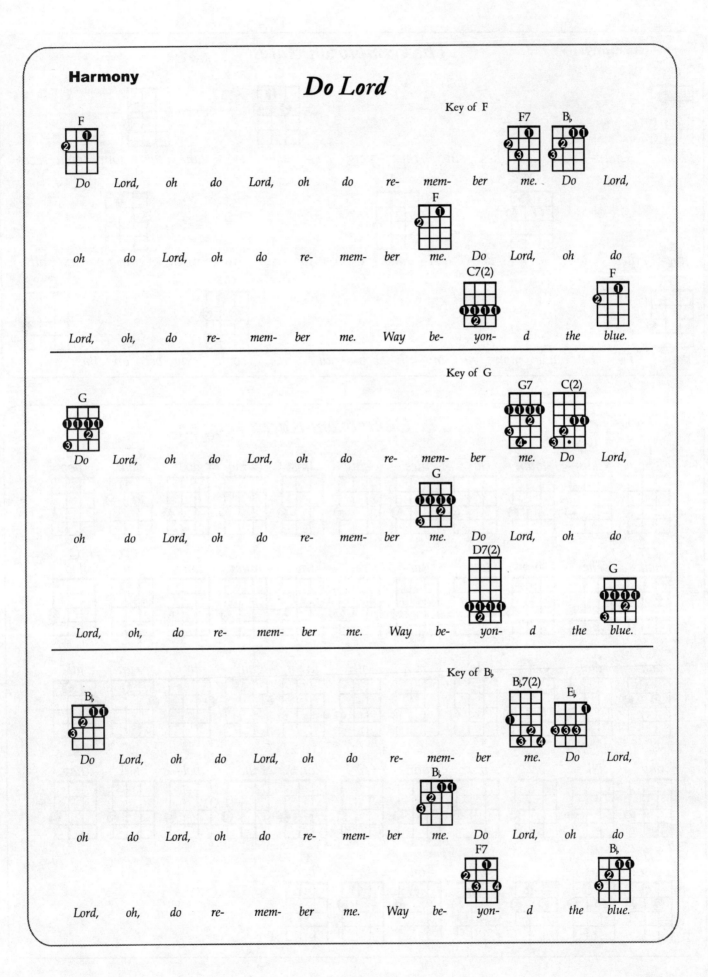

Key of F

F7 B♭

F

Do   Lord,   oh   do   Lord,   oh   do   re-   mem-   ber   me.   Do   Lord,

oh   do   Lord,   oh   do   re-   mem-   ber   me.   Do   Lord,   oh   do

C7(2)   F

Lord,   oh,   do   re-   mem-   ber   me.   Way   be-   yon-   d   the   blue.

Key of G

G7 C(2)

G

Do   Lord,   oh   do   Lord,   oh   do   re-   mem-   ber   me.   Do   Lord,

G

oh   do   Lord,   oh   do   re-   mem-   ber   me.   Do   Lord,   oh   do

D7(2)   G

Lord,   oh,   do   re-   mem-   ber   me.   Way   be-   yon-   d   the   blue.

Key of B♭

B♭7(2) E♭

B♭

Do   Lord,   oh   do   Lord,   oh   do   re-   mem-   ber   me.   Do   Lord,

B♭

oh   do   Lord,   oh   do   re-   mem-   ber   me.   Do   Lord,   oh   do

F7   B♭

Lord,   oh,   do   re-   mem-   ber   me.   Way   be-   yon-   d   the   blue.

Melody

Do Lord

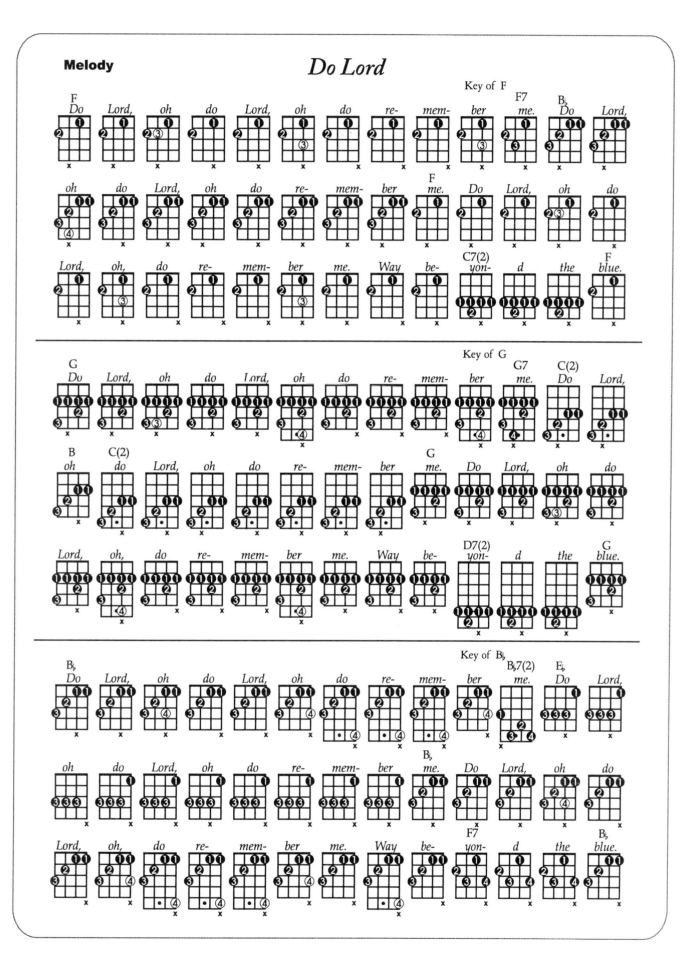

Harmony   *My Wild Irish Rose*   Key of B♭

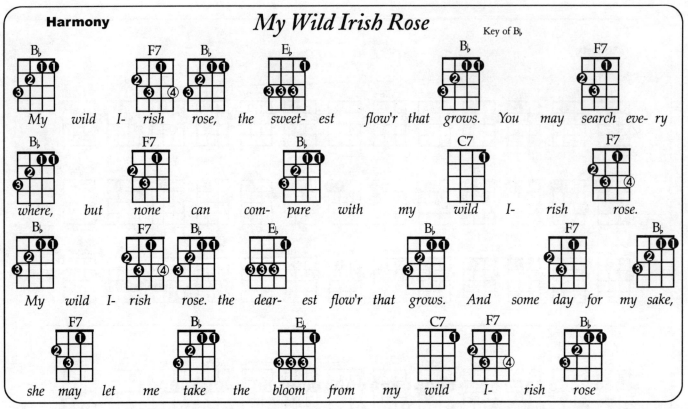

Melody   *My Wild Irish Rose*   Key of B♭

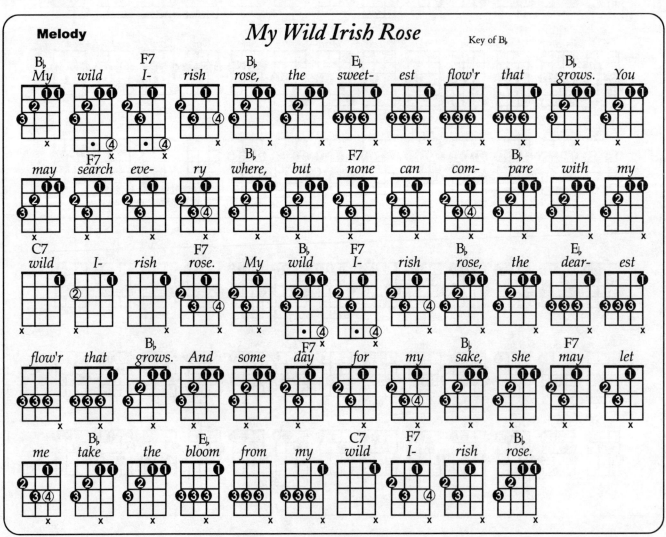

Harmony — *Swanee River* — Key of C

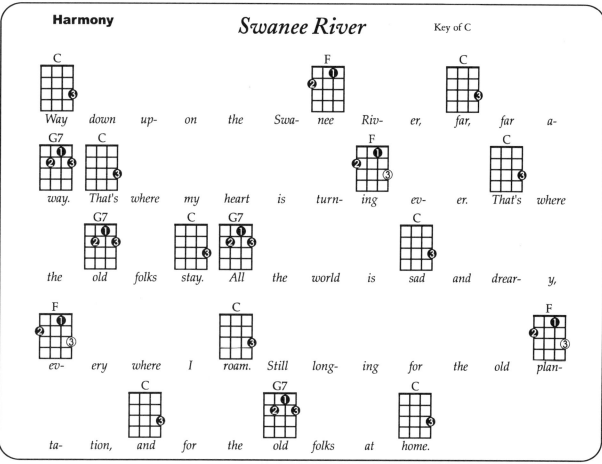

Melody — *Swanee River* — Key of C

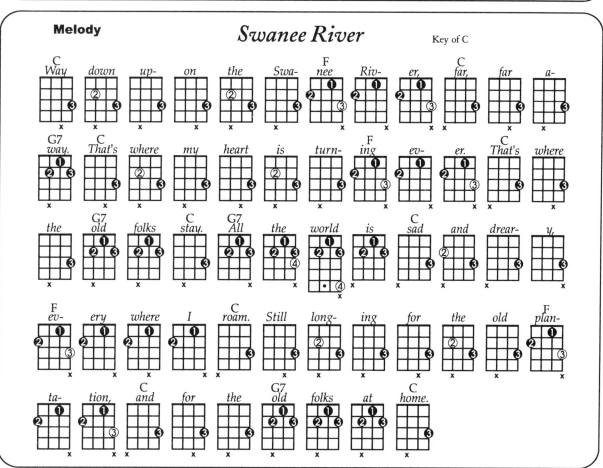

29

Swanee River

Harmony

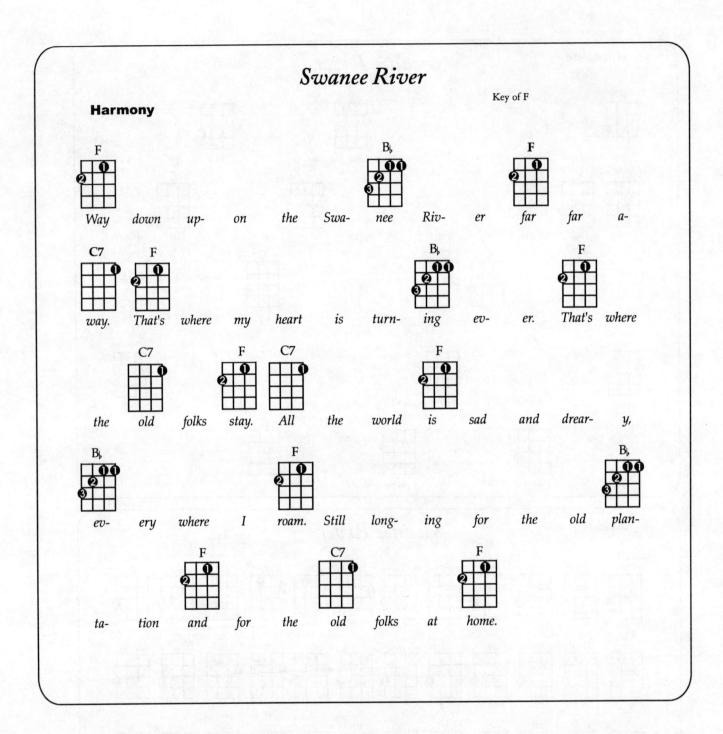

F					B♭			F			

Way   down   up-   on   the   Swa-   nee   Riv-   er   far   far   a-

C7   F   B♭   F

way.   That's   where   my   heart   is   turn-   ing   ev-   er.   That's   where

C7   F   C7   F

the   old   folks   stay.   All   the   world   is   sad   and   drear-   y,

B♭   F   B♭

ev-   ery   where   I   roam.   Still   long-   ing   for   the   old   plan-

F   C7   F

ta-   tion   and   for   the   old   folks   at   home.

Swanee River is used twice in the book because, when done in the **key of F,** it provides you an opportunity to use chords in **2nd**, **3rd** and even **4th** position.

Swanee River

Melody

Key of F

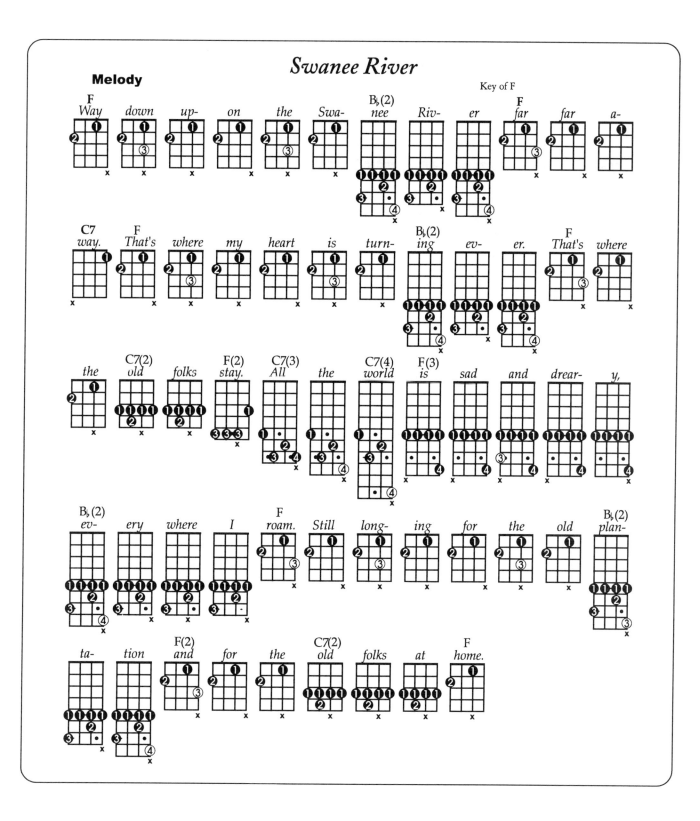

Harmony

When the Saints Go Marching In

Key of C

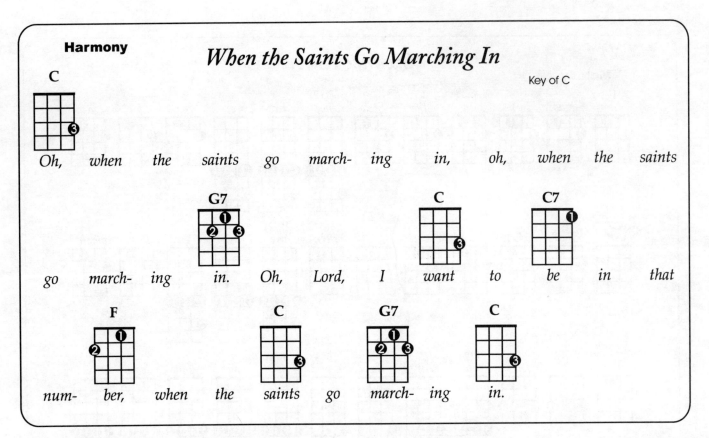

C

Oh, when the saints go march- ing in, oh, when the saints

G7 **C** **C7**

go march- ing in. Oh, Lord, I want to be in that

F **C** **G7** **C**

num- ber, when the saints go march- ing in.

Melody

When the Saints Go Marching In

Key of C

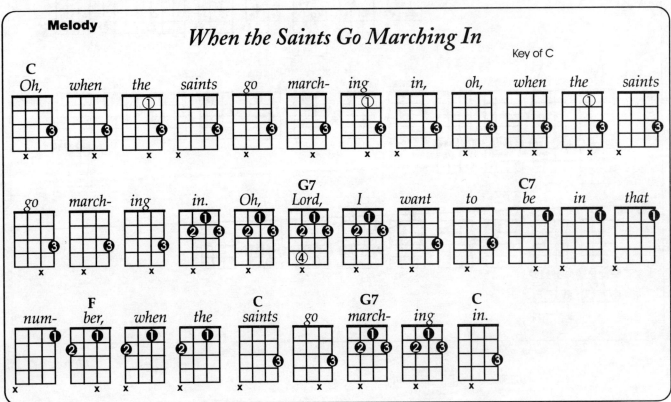

C

Oh, when the saints go march- ing in, oh, when the saints

go march- ing in. Oh, **G7** Lord, I want to **C7** be in that

F num- ber, when the **C** saints go **G7** march- ing **C** in.

32

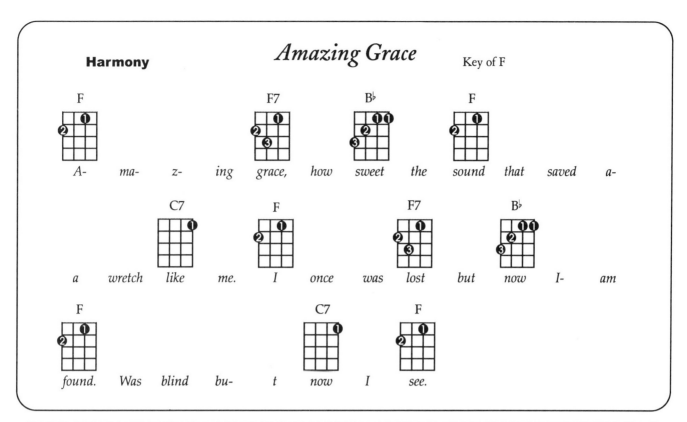

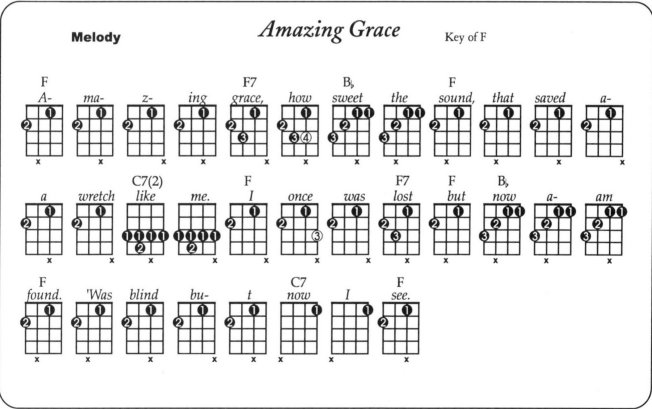

Amazing Grace, the final song in the book, was written by John Newton in the mid-1700s. He had been a slave ship captain, a "true wretch." After his ship nearly foundered in a storm, this lowly man changed his life, became a minister, and wrote hundreds of hymns, with this one being the most famous.

Chord Chart
Major Chords

A Chord
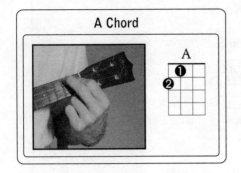

B♭ Chord
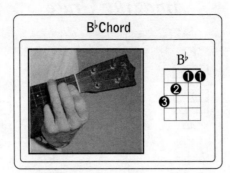

B Chord

C Chord
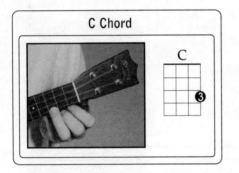

D♭ Chord
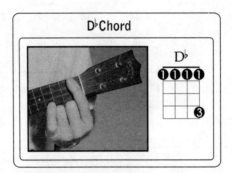

D Chord
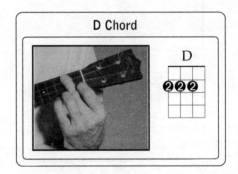

E♭ Chord
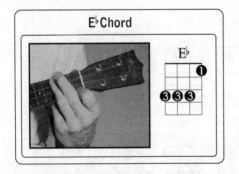

E Chord
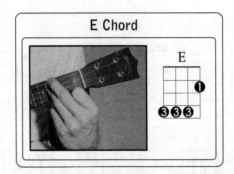

F Chord
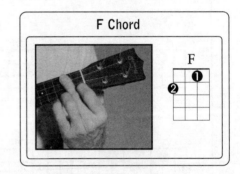

G♭ Chord
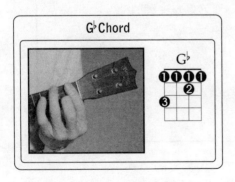

G Chord
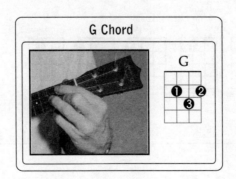

A♭ Chord
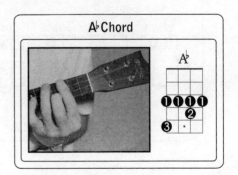

Chord Chart
Minor Chords

Am Chord
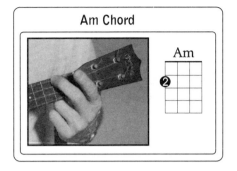

B♭m Chord
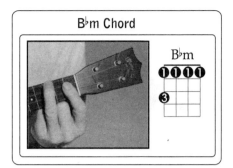

Bm Chord
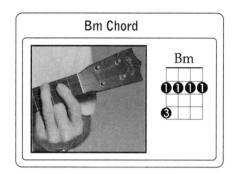

Cm Chord
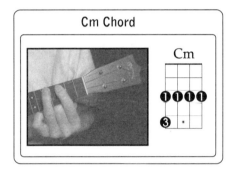

D♭m Chord
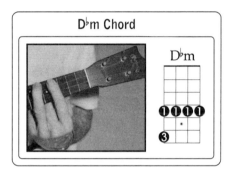

Dm Chord
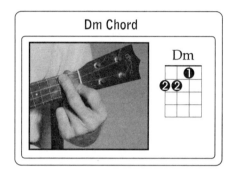

E♭m Chord

Em Chord
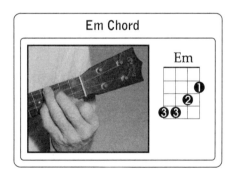

Fm Chord
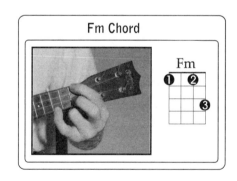

G♭m Chord
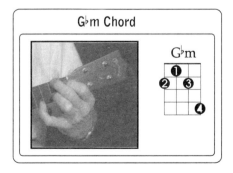

Gm Chord
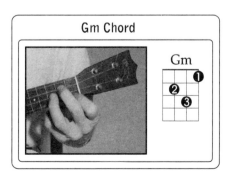

A♭m Chord
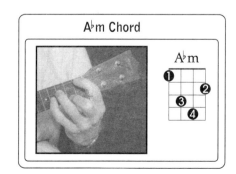

Chord Chart
Dominant Seventh Chords

A7 Chord
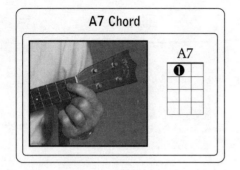

B♭7 Chord
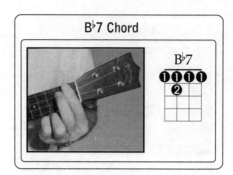

B7 Chord
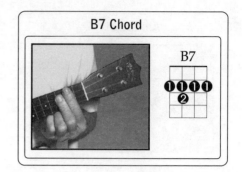

C7 Chord
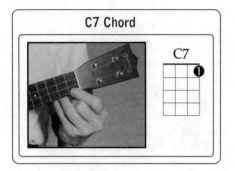

D♭7 Chord
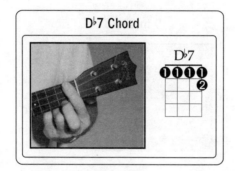

D7 Chord
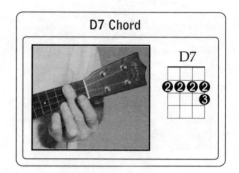

E♭7 Chord
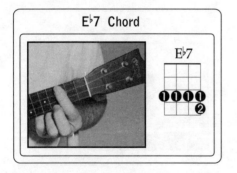

E7 Chord
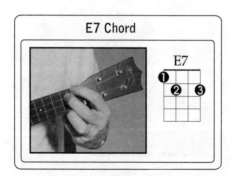

F7 Chord
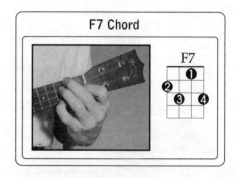

G♭7 Chord
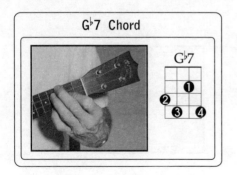

G7 Chord
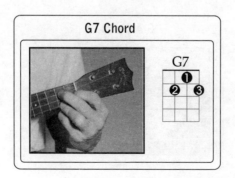

A♭7 Chord
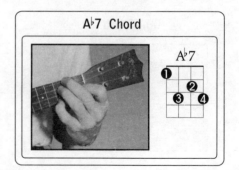

Key Chart
for GCEA Tuning

Key of A
A   D   E7

Key of B♭
B♭   E♭   F7

Key of B
B   E   G♭7

Key of C
C   F   G7

Key of D♭
D♭   G♭   A♭7

Key of D
D   G   A7

Key of E♭
E♭   A♭   B♭7

Key of E
E   A   B7

Key of F
F   B♭   C7

Key of G♭
G♭   B   D♭7

Key of G
G   C   D7

Key of A♭
A♭   D♭   E♭7

37

Chord Positions
Major Chords

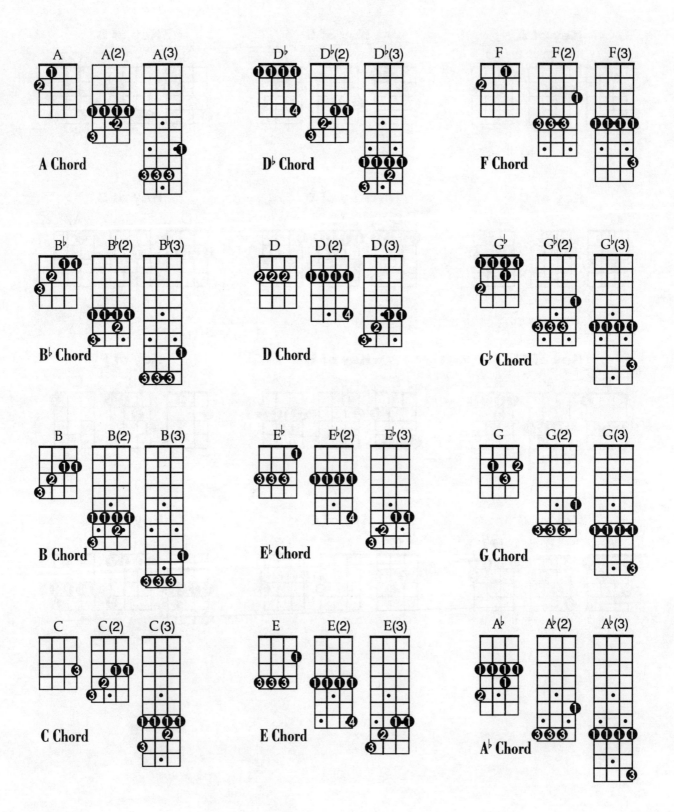

Chord Positions
Minor Chords

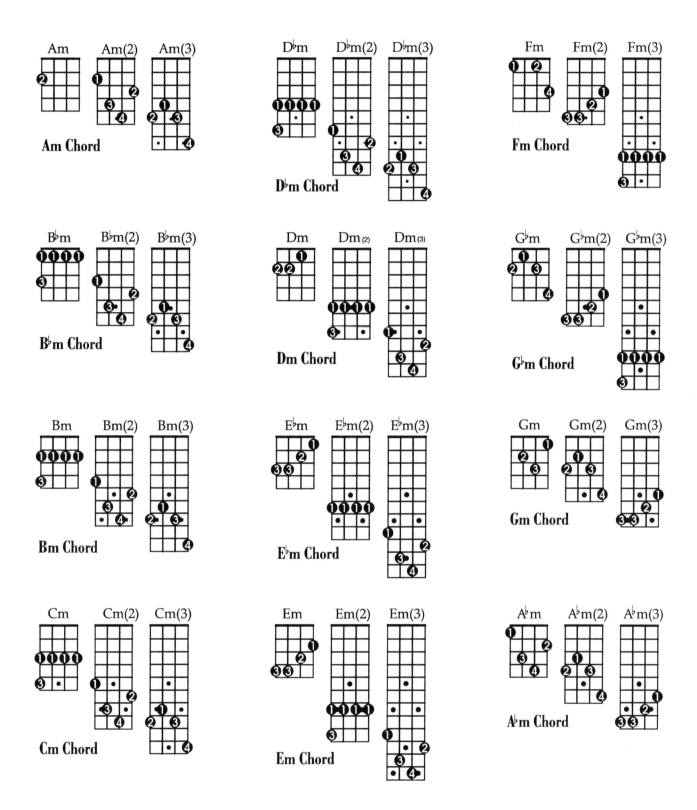

Chord Positions
Dominant Seventh Chords

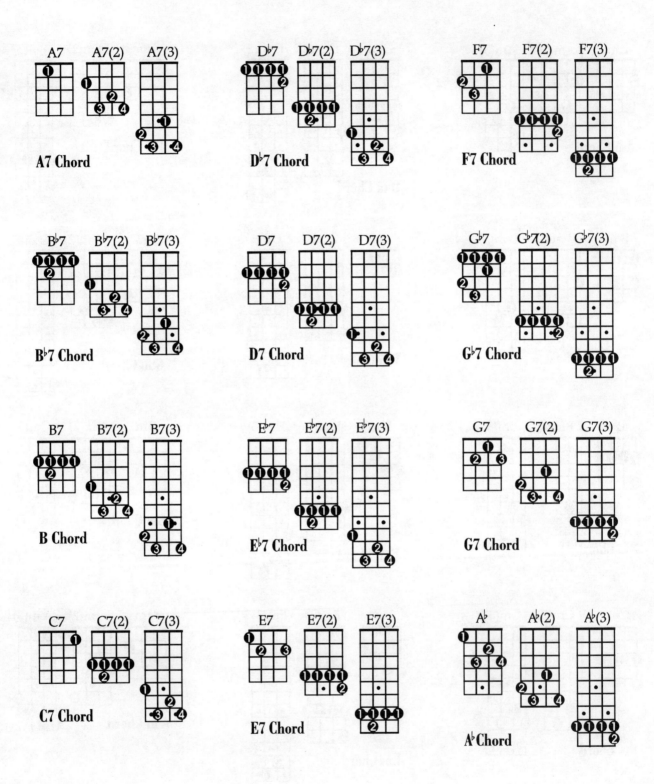